MW01101401

You Decide
Travel Guide
Loreto, Mexico

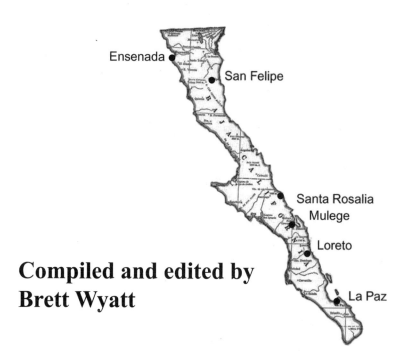

Ensenada
San Felipe
Santa Rosalia
Mulege
Loreto
La Paz

**Compiled and edited by
Brett Wyatt**

**Riley Books
Spokane, Washington**

You Decide Travel Guide:
Loreto, Mexico second edition

Cover Photo: Compliments of Hotel Posada de las Flores

Printed in the United States of America

Bulk purchases of You Decide Travel Guides are available for direct purchase at special discount pricing, and can be customized to fit the needs of your organization. For more information write to Bulk Sales, Riley Books, PO Box 8127, Spokane, WA 99203 or email

info@rileybooks.com

Riley Media Group LLC
Spokane, Washington 99203-0127

www.Rileybooks.com

ISBN 0-9708898-5-2

Dedication:
To the Girl

A note to our readers:

At Riley Books we strive to be accurate and up to date with our findings and to revise our guides as new facts present themselves. We cover a lot of ground in our books and if you should discover a mistake we would appreciate hearing from you. Please email your corrections or concerns to us at info@rileybooks.com.

Contents

Why another travel guide?

With dozens of companies publishing travel guides it is surprising to us that so many wonderful destinations have not received adequate coverage. At You Decide Travel Guide, we carefully select regions that have much to offer but generally only receive a few lines in other guides. Instead we feature an entire book that includes details on all of the local hotel properties and specific information about the local attractions with pricing and value facts.

Our Mission

To highlight areas with little or no coverage in other guides.

To provide a user friendly and helpful guide.

To go the extra mile in gathering information that you want to know.

How to use this travel guide.

When we offer options on how to get somewhere we always begin with what we consider the easiest mode of transport. Remember that the easiest way may not be the cheapest, but after that, we present a variety of other paths to your destination. Enough of our readers have an adventurous bent that we have sometimes included the more rugged routes for our more intrepid readers. For those of you who like to play it safe we give very detailed directions and always try to include prices.

Special Directions for using this guide:

We have also included a system of locating places in the area without complicated directions. Instead of giving long detailed directions we believe that in a small city like Loreto a simpler approach would handle this task. In addition to giving the address for use in case of traveling by taxi, and placing maps in the back, we also present your directions with the use of a clock symbol with a hand pointing in the direction of the establishment and a brief explanation of how far to go in that direction. In order to make this system work we needed to select a starting point. The graphic shown on the next page demonstrates this. For Loreto we give these directions from a starting point in front of the municipal building, facing the central plaza towards the Sea of Cortez to the east. That is the building pictured on the facing page. For those of you who just read that and said, "WHAT?" we also offer the "old standby," map of the city, with locations of hotels and restaurants marked and numbered.

**This would mean
that this location
is 7 blocks from
the point in front
of the municipal
bldg.**

**Start here
facing in
the direction
of the arrow**

**Follow directions
from this point.**

⌘⌘ Our writers ran into the owners of more than one hotel who insisted that their hotel was only a couple of blocks from downtown because there were only two cross streets on the way. In fact it was nearly a kilometer. For this reason we have found it necessary to offer our definition of a block.

Block: a measure of length usually approximately 12 to a mile or 7.5 to a kilometer. This varies a bit, but offers a good baseline.

$$$$ Ratings ?????

This book delivers a large amount of detailed information and while we do tell you when we like something and why, our focus is on giving you the information necessary to decide. We don't give a sales pitch, instead we deliver the facts that give you the power not to be manipulated by sales pitches and gimmicks.

For every hotel property we give the most up to date pricing information available. If we ever find a property to be way out of line in its pricing versus what it delivers then we will offer that thought in the "Final Word" portion on that hotel.

Why Loreto?

Loreto is an unspoiled destination just over 1100 kilometers south of San Diego. There are over 240 kilometers of coastline and the beautiful Sierra La Giganta mountain range lies behind Loreto. The area is home to one of Mexico's national marine parks. These parks are dedicated to preserving the amazing sea life that prospers here while allowing people to visit and interact with it. This definitely isn't Cabo and it isn't meant to be. It is a quiet little town that can stand for a bit more excitement, but not too much. The thing is, that more excitement won't come to Loreto until there are more people but it is hard to get more people without the excitement. So Loreto will keep growing at its own pace and welcomes tourists to share in that growth.

Loreto is home to what many say is the best fishing in all of Mexico. For those who prefer to explore underneath the sea, the clear, warm water hosts close to 3,000 species of sea life. For those who prefer land sports, there is a 18 hole championship golf course right on the sea. Just a few blocks from the golf course is the Nopolo Professional Tennis Center. There are 8 courts and a pool and sauna as well.

You can rent A.T.V.'s or a sea kayak. The options are only limited by your imagination. In the evenings there is a wide selection of dining establishments all serving classic Mexican drinks. Wake up the next day for shopping or more exploring.

Enjoy your trip to Loreto.

History of the Area:

In 1697 Juan Maria Salvatierra established the first settlement in California when he founded the Our Lady of Loreto Mission. For 133 years Loreto served as the capital of California. During these years the mission system in California was greatly expanded. Father Junipero Serra was the driving force in the founding of 17 missions reaching up to modern central California. Father Salvatierra continued his work in southern Baja. They contin-

ued their work until 1768 when Carlos III of Spain expelled all members of the Society of Jesus (Jesuits) from all Spanish possessions. In 1829 a hurricane destroyed much of the town and fear of future storms caused the government to move the capital 230 kilometers south to La Paz. For a time the area remained largely unin- habited but in the 1850's the area was settled. A number of foreigners including some from England were among these settlers. The next hundred years allowed Loreto to disappear in great measure from the notice of Mexico's neighbors to the north. The 1940's brought the be- ginnings of what would become a large sportsfishing indus- try that now draws people from around the world. It wasn't until the early 1970's when the Transpeninsular Highway (Route 1) was completed from Tijuana to Cabo San Lucas, that Loreto was embraced by people outside of the fishing mainstream.

Tourists began to trickle down and as more of them make their way to Loreto an increasing number of services become available and make this a destination to watch.

Climate:

Over 360 days of sunshine make
this region a perfect escape from the win-
ter months up north. The area's climate
is dry and after you leave the oasis area
created by civilization you will find yourself traveling through desert. The tem-
perature can drop below freezing at night
but can and does exceed 100 degrees Fahrenheit during the
day in the summer.

Average High Temperatures:

January:	high 60's F - low 70's F
February:	high 60's F - low 70's F
March:	low 70's F
April:	mid 70's F
May:	low 80's F
June:	mid 80's F
July:	low 90's F
August:	low 90's F - mid 90's F
September:	mid 90's F
October:	mid 90's F
November:	mid 80's F
December:	low 70's F - mid 70's F

The Journey:

Getting to Loreto and back again

By far the easiest way to Loreto is by plane. Loreto has a wonderful airport capable of landing most commercial and private aircraft. The airport is just 5 kilometers from the central plaza in Loreto.

Alaska Airlines will begin offering twice weekly service on February 17 of 2005. These flights will be between Loreto and Los Angeles and will occur on Thursdays and Sundays.

U.S.A. Phone	1-800-252-7522
Website:	www.alaskaair.com

AeroCalifornia offers non-stop air service from Los Angeles.

U.S.A. Phone	1-800-524-9191
Loreto Airport Office:	(613) 135 0555
Loreto City Office:	(613) 135 0500

AeroMexico offers Service from San Diego.

U.S.A. Phone	1-800-237-6639
Loreto Airport	(613) 135 0999
Website:	www.aeromexico.com

AeroLitoral is a regional partner airline of AeroMexico and offers daily service from Los Angeles with a stop in Hermosillo. Planes are 33 passenger prop planes so they take a bit longer to deliver you to Loreto.

Phone and contacts the same as AeroMexico.

Arriving in Mexico, the flight crew passes out immigration and customs forms.

One of these is the customs declaration (aduana Mexico). It includes information on what you are bringing with you as you enter Mexico including live animals, fruits & vegetables and large sums of cash. Be sure to check customs regulations before you leave home to avoid problems.

The other is the immigration form, or as they say the Migratory Form for Foreign Tourist, TRANSMIGRANT. This is a two part form with the top half being used for entry into Mexico.

The bottom half is returned to you and you keep it until your departure. Think of it as your ticket out of Mexico. If you lose, it you are in for hassles in the form of paperwork, delays and at last check a penalty of $45 USD for replacement. It is a good idea to keep it with your passport for safe keeping.

Arriving at the Airport:

Down the portable stairs and a three - five minute walk gets you into the terminal building. Through immigration, (the aduana) and then a quick stop to press the customs button to see if you get the green light (Red light means you are lucky enough to have your bags searched). Then it is out into the wonderful world of securing transit to Loreto, or wherever you might be going. A couple of hotels offer complimentary shuttle service from the airport, but for most, plan on paying for a shuttle van. The price is about $8 USD a person, usually quoted in pesos, but they should have change if you are carrying small bills.

Alaska Airlines has established a reputation for excellent service since it's inception in 1932. First flying to Mexico in 1988, they are as much as anyone responsible for the growth and development of Los Cabos and other resort destinations in Mexico. Their planes are clean and their staff very courteous. Upgrades to first class are available at the gate for only $50. While the flight is less than two hours, who can resist a comfortable, wide seat and the special treatment that comes along with sitting up front. For now, two flights a week depart out of Los Angeles, but as demand increases the flights will as well. A+ for Alaska Airlines

Driving to Loreto from the U.S.

Loreto is approximately 1100 kilometers from the U.S. border. The main highway in Baja (Transpeninsular #1) is well maintained but sometimes narrow. You will need to have additional auto insurance as most policies exempt travel into Mexico. Driving your car into Mexico more than 20 kilometers usually requires a temporary vehicle importation permit. When traveling exclusively into Baja California or Baja California Sur this requirement is waived unless you plan on traveling to the mainland via ferry.

•Be patient, and expect delays at the border or at the occasional roadblock where they search for drugs or other illegal things. Also, there are tolls associated with this route. Just make sure they are collecting the posted amount.

•Make sure that you pack emergency supplies. When driving in Mexico it is also a good idea to pack some tools and possibly some common auto parts.

•Get a good map before you leave so that you know where services including gas, food and lodging are.

•Your options for gas are limited to Pemex gas stations which take only cash or the GasoPLUS credit card.

Travel into La Paz and then to Loreto:

It is 230 kilometers to Loreto from the La Paz airport. Your choices include taking a half hour charter flight from La Paz direct to Loreto, or make the trip by car or bus.

Cars are available from several companies that you should recognize from home. This might be a good option if you are planning on returning to La Paz, as there are currently only two rental offices in Loreto. Which generally makes one way rentals not a workable option.

Several buses daily operate from La Paz to Loreto and take about 4 1/2 hours to make the trip. The cost is 249 pesos or about $22 USD. The buses are comfortable with air conditioning and occasionally, movies. They do stop along the way for passengers and to give the opportunity to make snack purchases

Visit Loreto on a Cruise:

At this time, three cruise lines offer Loreto as a seasonal port of call. One is Holland America, which offers cruises out of southern California. Another cruise line is CruiseWest, which offers smaller ships and features trips out of Cabo San Lucas. They offer voyages that bring passengers up close to whales and other sea life. Finally, there is American Safari Cruises, which offers itself as a provider of exclusive yacht adventures. The trips that include Loreto on the itinerary leave from San Jose del Cabo. These yachts hold from 18-24 passengers.

Contact Information for Cruise Providers:

Holland America: www.hollandamerica.com
CruiseWest: www.cruisewest.com
American Safari Cruises: www.amsafari.com

From Los Cabos:

If you are driving, plan for 580 kilometers on a narrow winding highway through the mountains.   It is recommended that you only travel during the day and plan for a several hour trip.

If you are traveling by bus and make good connections your trip should last about 10 hours. The cost is 373 pesos or about $34 USD. The bus station is in Cabo San Lucas and can be reached by taxi or by hiking out to the highway and taking a local bus.

From Tijuana:

The bus trip lasts about 14 hours.   The central bus terminal in Tijuana (Centro de Autobuses) is where most long distance bus services depart from including Autotransportes A.B.C. and Autotransportes del Pacifico.

Local Activites
& Fun

Activities

The Beach:

There is a small public beach on the north end of the malecon. There are several palapas there for your use. The beaches seem to get lighter in color and softer as you get further from town, but they all have beautiful views.

South of Loreto about 21 kilometers is Playa Juncalita which is a beach enclave where many snowbirds keep palapas for their R.V.s. Keep heading south and you will arrive at Ensenada Blanca.

Continuing south on the transpeninsular highway will bring you to as much beach as you can handle. Just bring enough water for your trip as there are some stretches of road without civilization for many kilometers.

Fishing:

Try to make your own record catch in the Sea of Cortez. There is no shortage of companies wanting to take you out on a fishing trip. There are dozens of local boats to rent, with or without a crew. You can also bring yours from home. With the area protected from commercial fishing many believe that this is the best fishing in Baja.

Companies offering Boats or Tours:

Arturos Sport Fishing Fleet:
    from U.S.A. 011 52 (613) 135-0766
    www.arturosport.com

The Baja Big Fish Company:
    from U.S.A. 011 52 (613) 135-1603

Oasis Sport Fishing:

    from U.S.A. 011 52 (613) 135-0211

Ricardo's Sport Fishing:
    from U.S.A. 011 52 (613) 135-0126
    office at La Pinta Hotel

Annual Fishing Seasons:

Dorado:	May through September
Blue Marlin:	July through September
Striped Marlin:	March and April
Sailfish:	June through September
Sierra:	November through February
Jack:	February through May
Tuna:	June through September
Yellowtail:	February through May
Rooster Fish:	October through April
Cabrilla:	March through June
Red Snapper:	March through June
Grouper:	February through April and October & November

<u>Activities</u>

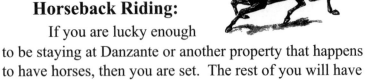

Horseback Riding:

If you are lucky enough
to be staying at Danzante or another property that happens
to have horses, then you are set. The rest of you will have
to go through one of the tour agencies to hire your ride.

One company that offers horseback tours or who can
arrange horse rental is Las Parras Tours at
011 52 (613) 135 1010 or at
Guaycura Adventours at 135 1378 or cell
phone (613) 104 3581

Scuba Diving and Snorkeling:

The water near Loreto rises to nearly 90
degrees Fahrenheit in the summer and fall. The
visibility ranges from 40 to over 140 feet. In
the spring, though, the visibility can be far less. Of 3,000
species of aquatic life, over 800 varieties of fish reside off of
Loreto in the sea. There are many tour operators who offer
diving packages and equipment.

One of these companies is Las Parras Tours which is
just a block off the central plaza at Hidalgo and Madera. Their
telephone number is 135 1010 or email them at
tourloreto@aol.com or lasparras@prodigy.net.mx.

Another option is Dolphin Dive Center which is located
on site at Villas de Loreto. They are a full service dive shop
and can handle your repair needs for diving equipment as
well as renting anything that you might need. They have a
U.S.A. contact number of (626) 484-9408 or email them at
info@dolphindivebaja.com.   Their   website   is
www.dolphindivebaja.com.

<u>Activities</u>

El Campo del Golf

(18 hole professional course)

They are working very hard to finish the landscaping for this course that has several challenging holes, including one that tees off from high above a bluff then goes over water to the hole. The prices are very good. At last check they were only $25 to play 18 holes for guests of the Camino Real. For those who are not guests of the hotel, the price for 18 holes is $40.

Nopolo Tennis Center:

This magnificent tennis complex has eight courts including one in an auditorium setting for matches in front of your 200 friends that came to Loreto with you. It is located in Nopolo up the road from the Camino Real. If you are going to be playing tennis a lot then you might want to look into staying in Nopolo. It is open daily from 7 am - 11 pm.

Court Rental is $8 USD per hour
Court lighting is $10 USD per hour
Racquet Rental $5 USD & includes use of three balls
Swimming Pool Fee $5 USD

The complex is well maintained and the trees offer some shade from the Mexican sun. As it is near the sea there is also a breeze that comes through quite a bit of the time.

Activities

Mountain Biking:

A bike makes a tour of the city a breeze, and if you want to venture out beyond the boundaries of Loreto, you have many options. It is a 37 km ride into the mountains to San Javier. The highway isn't very wide so be very careful, especially if you see a big truck. Once you turn off of the highway towards San Javier the biggest challenge is making it up the mountain. Just look west if you are wondering where to ride. You will see the Sierra Gigante and the foothills which are near Loreto.

Check the websites for hotels that offer bikes for their guests. If you want to rent a bike, Las Parras Tours offers rentals by the hour, half day and full day. They also offer guided bike tours.

You can contact them at 011 52 (613) 135 1010

If you are going to ride out of town you should pack enough water, and it is a good idea to buy a map so that you can find your way back to enjoy another day in Loreto.

If you need bicycle repairs or supplies there is a pretty good bike shop in town owned by Manni. It is on the map in the back. Manni also is part of the local bike club and can tell you about the races that are held in Baja.

<u>Activities</u>

A.T.V. Rental

Moto Tours which has offices at La Pinta Hotel and at the Budget rent a car office. Rent A.T.V.'s by the hour or the day. Their phone number at La Pinta is 011 52 (613) 135 1090.

The Motel El Dorado also has A.T.V.'s for rent. Their phone number from the U.S. is (888) 314-9023 or from Loreto is 135 1700.

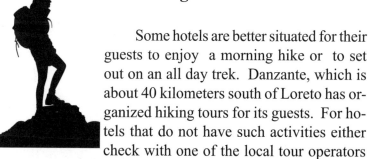

Hiking:

Some hotels are better situated for their guests to enjoy a morning hike or to set out on an all day trek. Danzante, which is about 40 kilometers south of Loreto has organized hiking tours for its guests. For hotels that do not have such activities either check with one of the local tour operators or fill your rucksack with enough to drink and any other supplies you might need. If you drive to your trailhead then you should be able to find your way back to town as long as you pay some attention to your direction. With the hills resting as they do to the west, then a quick check of landmarks before you leave sight of town and a map should keep you on track. The trip to the cave paintings north of town actually requires quite a bit of hiking so that trip might be a good idea if you have some energy to burn.

<u>Activities</u>

Kayaking:

The local tour operators offer sea kayak tours and many hotels either rent them out or offer them free for guests. Many people come to Loreto for the tours offered and enjoy the protected areas from sea level. The sea off Loreto is generally calm unless the wind really picks up, so even someone starting out should be able to enjoy this activity.

Many adventurers paddle across the sea to one of the islands and camp out for a day or two. Make sure that you bring adequate equipment and supplies though, as there are no services on the islands.

Whalewatching:

Each year,   thousands of gray whales make the trip from the north to the waters off of western Baja to give birth to their young and to then make the journey back north-ward again. The time for viewing them begins in January and lasts through March. The location closest to Loreto that gives you the best chance of seeing these wonderous animals, comes at Lopez Mateos which is about 130 kilometers away. There are many tour companies offering this trip once you get down to Loreto or if that is the reason for your trip to Baja, you may want to book this excursion before you arrive in Loreto.

<u>Activities</u>

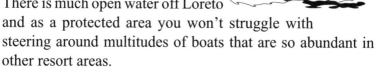

Wind Surfing

We haven't found a way to rent wind surfing equipment in Loreto yet but those who bring their own kayaks surely could fit a wind surfing outfit on top of their cars as well. There is much open water off Loreto and as a protected area you won't struggle with steering around multitudes of boats that are so abundant in other resort areas.

Boating:

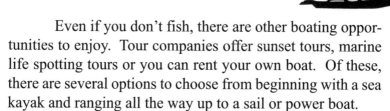

Even if you don't fish, there are other boating opportunities to enjoy. Tour companies offer sunset tours, marine life spotting tours or you can rent your own boat. Of these, there are several options to choose from beginning with a sea kayak and ranging all the way up to a sail or power boat.

The waters off of Loreto make for some great sailing and there is plenty of room to navigate while still staying within sight of the town.

Activities

Shopping:

Loreto has got this down. Calle Salvatierra runs east-west past the central plaza and the mission. This street was designed to be a shopping corridor with shops featuring everything from T-shirts to souvenirs and the work of local artisans. This corridor will eventually feature shops from the malecon all the way past the mission for several blocks. They have added sculpted landscape arches over the street. The streets on either side of, and crossing Calle Salvatierra also feature shops that should not be ignored.

The Public Library:

The public library is about 20 meters from the municipal building on the central plaza. It is on the first floor of a two story building and has a collection of a few thousand books. They have recently painted the outside of the building, and like the rest of Loreto it is getting upgraded. Most of the books are in Spanish and they only allow residents to check out books, but if you need to brush up on your written spanish, what better way than to spend an afternoon in the library. The librarian does her best to understand English but you will be better off with at least a little Spanish if asking for help.

A little bit of Romance:

Horse drawn carriage rides:
Call 011 52 (613) 135-0967

Their flyer advertises an amazing 100 pesos an hour rate. That is less than $10 USD. Whether for social events, evening rides along the malecon, or for any outing this seems like a good bet.

Video Games:

There are several video gaming establishments in Loreto. Most are small and have older games, but if you are bored and tired of cave paintings, fishing or the beach this could provide a distraction.   Some of these include air hockey, foosball and a couple also offer Playstation and Nintendo Stations for rent by the half hour. The arcade games cost just one peso each so a few bucks will last the day if you are careful.

If nothing else, at least it is an air-conditioned escape from the hot sun, and they do serve snacks.

Activities

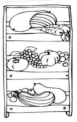

Que Buena Fruteria:

Three stores west from the intersection of Benito Juarez and Francisco Madero brings you to a large fruit shop. It is covered and features the largest fruit selection we found in Loreto.

Movie Theater:

Word on the street is that a movie theater is in the works for Loreto. A developer has purchased property and is looking to build. Keep an eye out, hopefully the next months will make this a reality.

The Local Pool Hall:

Located near the corner of Heroes Independencia y Calle Independencia.

This is a serious local's hangout. It has 5 pool tables that cost 15 pesos an hour for the table. The manager said tourists are welcome and they serve chips and soft drinks.

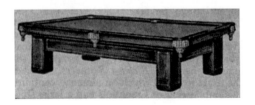

Hotels & Lodging

Hotel Classifications

Beach Front   (All Classes)

Camino Real
Danzante
Hotel Oasis
La Pinta Hotel
Loreto Playa B & B
Villas de Loreto
Whales Inn

Non-Beach Front
(Moderate and up)

Coco Cabanas
Hacienda Suites
Hotel Quinta San Francisco
Iguana Inn
Olive Tree Villas
SuKasa

Ultra Budget
(A roof over your head)

Motel Brenda
Motel Salvatierra
Hotel Posada San Martin
Hotel Palmas Altas

Non-Beach Front   (Deluxe)

Posada de las Flores

Budget Properties
(Save $$ and still get an okay room)

Hotel Plaza Loreto
Hotel Junipero
El Moro Motel and R.V. Park
Motel El Dorado

Closed   (may open again)

La Mision de Loreto
Las Trojes

Ultra-budget

Motel Brenda

Ave. Juarez s/n Loreto,
B.C.S. 23880 Mexico

Phone: 011 52 (613) 135 07 07 **Fax:** 011 52 (613) 135 0707

Date Last Remodeled: 1993
A Word About Location:

This motel is on the fringes of downtown in a non-tourist neighborhood. It is only six blocks from the central plaza. There are many colorful local eateries in the surrounding blocks. Most of these restaurants are the road side stand variety or family operated units in special additions to houses. They cater to locals and the occasional wandering tourist.

Facility Description:

There are 17 rooms, twelve of which have a double bed and a twin bed. Five rooms have one queen bed. The sign says hot water 24 hours a day and it was when we checked. There is a convenience store and liquor store next door as well.

Rates		
1 Person	**2 Persons**	**3 Persons**
220 Pesos	**250 Pesos**	**280 Pesos**
currently	**currently**	**currently**
$ 22 USD	**$25 USD**	**$28 USD**

All Prices + 12% tax

Promotions: None

Credit Card Acceptance: None

Air Conditioning	Satellite / Cable TV	Telephone in Room	Swimming Pool	Jacuzzi	Non Smoking Rooms	Wheelchair Access	Kitchenette	Refrigerator	Microwave	In Room Coffee	Continental Breakfast	On-Site Restaurant	On-Site Store	Lighted Parking
X	X													

Beach	Golf Nearby	Elevator	Dead Bolt Locks	Pets Okay	Meeting Rooms	Balconies	Banquet Facility	Cribs Available	Child Care	In Room Safe	Room Service	Interior Corridors	Exterior Corridors	24 Hr. Security
			X										X	

The Final Word:

Cheap room that has a lock on the door. It is a bit dusty in the parking lot, but it is a roof over your head.

New tile on outdoor hallways

10 Kilometers

Beachfront property

Camino Real

Blvd. Mision de Loreto s/n.
Fracc. Nopolo, 23880
Loreto, B.C.S.Mexico

Website: www.Caminoreal.com   E-Mail: Ltosales@caminoreal.com

Phone: 011 52 (613) 133 0010   Fax: 011 52 (613) 133 0020

Date Opened: February 15, 2002

A Word About Location:

The Camino Real is situated in Nopolo, a neighborhood 10 km from downtown Loreto or about a 10 minute taxi ride. There are plans for shopping and restaurants but for now if you want fun beyond the walls of the Camino Real you need to make the trip into Loreto. While city exploration does require more work on your part this property allows for relaxation free from crowds or other random city distractions.

Facility Description:

There is lots of room everywhere in the hotel. From the lobby through the halls and even in the bathrooms there is room to stretch. There are two restaurants and a poolside snack shack which offers hot food and drinks. The 155 rooms are outfitted with large color TV's, powerful air conditioning and each has a great view of the Sea of Cortez. A walk through of the kitchen facility finds an immaculate area on par with the finest hotel anywhere. The dining room serves wonderful food at surprisingly fair prices. Child care available upon request.

Rates		
Deluxe ocean view room	$145 USD	
Junior Suite Terrace	$195 USD	extra persons
Master Suite Jacuzzi	$235 USD	after two $30

——— All Prices + 12% tax ———

Promotions: Check website
Credit Card Acceptance: MasterCard, Visa

Air Conditioning	Satellite / Cable TV	Telephone in Room	Swimming Pool	Jacuzzi	Non Smoking Rooms	Wheelchair Access	Kitchenette	Refrigerator	Microwave	In Room Coffee	Continental Breakfast	On-Site Restaurant	On-Site Store	Lighted Parking
X	X	X	X	X	X			X			X	X	X	

Beach	Golf Nearby	Elevator	Dead Bolt Locks	Pets Okay	Meeting Rooms	Balconies	Banquet Facility	Cribs Available	Child Care	In Room Safe	Room Service	Interior Corridors	Exterior Corridors	24 Hr. Security
X	X	X	X		X	X	X	X	X	X	X		X	X

The Final Word:

They have a full array of activities including basketball, sea kayaks, a fitness center, mountain bikes, a golf course, tennis center nearby and a wonderful pool and beach area

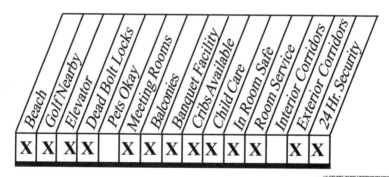

The nicest full service beach front hotel in the area

6 blocks

Moderate +

Coco Cabanas

Calle Davis
Loreto, B.C.S. 23880 Mexico

Website: www.CocoCabanasLoreto.com E-Mail: barrett@coco-cabanas.com

Phone: 011 52 (613) 135 1729   Cell: 011 44 (613) 104 2264

Date Opened: May 2002

A Word About Location:

West off of Calle Davis, just a stone's throw from the malecon you will find this group of Cabanas surrounding a lovely courtyard with a pool in the center. When you leave the property you walk down about a block to Calle Davis and turn right and then right again at the corner for a quick walk to the north end of the Malecon. Turn left off of Calle Davis to walk to the central plaza.

Facility Description:

Eight air conditioned cabanas with TVs and VCRs as well as a free video library. Each unit has a kitchen with a stove, refrigerator, microwave and is stocked with dishes and cookware. There is also a dining table in each of these clean and well built accomodations. Two of the cabanas have a double bed and two bunk beds. The remaining six have one double bed and a twin. Just out of the door of each cabana are chairs and a table to enjoy an evening drink and a few feet more brings you to the pool area that has lounge chairs for reading and laying in the sun. A barbecue and newly built fish cleaning station are also available for the use of guests.

All cabanas are $60 a night
$350/ week   third adult add $10
prices are for one or two adults, under 12 free

All Prices + 12% tax

Promotions: Check website

Credit Card Acceptance: MasterCard & Visa via paypal

Air Conditioning	Satellite / Cable TV	Telephone in Room	Swimming Pool	Jacuzzi	Non Smoking Rooms	Wheelchair Access	Kitchenette	Refrigerator	Microwave	In Room Coffee	Continental Breakfast	On-Site Restaurant	On-Site Store	Lighted Parking
X		X			X	X	X	X						X

Beach	Golf Nearby	Elevator	Dead Bolt Locks	Pets Okay	Meeting Rooms	Balconies	Banquet Facility	Cribs Available	Child Care	In Room Safe	Room Service	Interior Corridors	Exterior Corridors	24 Hr. Security
		X	X										X	

The Final Word:

Coco Cabanas is very clean and quiet; a retreat that many will find themselves returning to. A hidden jewel in Loreto.

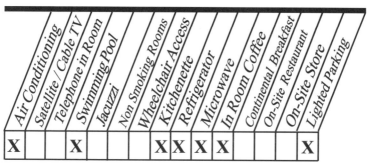

When you need some quiet rest and a clean room

44 Kilometers

Beachfront property

Danzante

PO Box 1166
Los Gatos, CA 95031

Website: www.danzante.com   **E-mail:** info@danzante.com
Phone: (408) 354-0042 USA   **Fax:** (408) 354-3268 USA

A Word About Location:

40 kilometers south of Loreto you will find a 10 acre seaside resort in a secluded bay on the Sea of Cortez. Located within the boundaries of the Loreto National Marine Park, this location offers incredible views and terrain while still being close to Loreto and the airport.

Facility Description:

9 junior suites make up this all inclusive Mexican style ranch like facility. This 100% solar powered resort targets those interested in eco-tourism and delivers with an amazing array of activities. The management works hard to keep a harmony with nature and the local population. A look at their website offers a more detailed look at just how they accomplish this. All rooms are non-smoking and they have horseback riding, kayaking and a secluded beach for swimming and snorkeling. The facilities and service are excellent.

Rates

All inclusive Per Person / Double Occupancy
$145-195 per person double occupancy
includes breakfast / lunch / dinner

——————— All Prices + 15% tax ———————

Payment terms: 30% deposit required

Promotions: Check website
Credit Card Acceptance: MasterCard & Visa

Air Conditioning	Satellite / Cable TV	Telephone in Room	Swimming Pool	Jacuzzi	Non Smoking Rooms	Wheelchair Access	Kitchenette	Refrigerator	Microwave	In Room Coffee	Continental Breakfast	On-Site Restaurant	On-Site Store	Lighted Parking
		X		X								X		

Beach	Golf Nearby	Elevator	Dead Bolt Locks	Pets Okay	Meeting Rooms	Balconies	Banquet Facility	Cribs Available	Child Care	In Room Safe	Room Service	Interior Corridors	Exterior Corridors	24 Hr. Security
X													X	

The Final Word:

Danzante is an all-inclusive eco-tourism resort that takes getting close to nature, but not harming it to a new level. Also don't miss the daily margarita party.

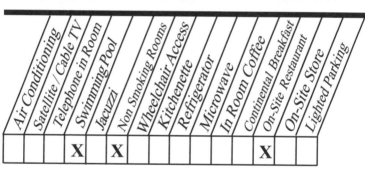

The only true eco-resort in the area.

Motel El Dorado

3 Blocks

Budget

Located at Paseo Miguel Hidalgo
and Pipila   Loreto, B.C.S. 23880
Mexico

Website: www.moteleldorado.com **E-mail** info@moteleldorado.com
Phone: 011 52 (613) 135 1500   **Fax:** 011 52 (613) 135 1700
Phone Toll Free from US: (800) 314-9023

A Word About Location:

Two blocks from the central plaza and situated in a residential area, the El Dorado is a great location for access to town and to the sea.

Facility Description:

This motel is 1/2 block off a main road down a dirt street, and makes these 11 rooms around a central bar perfect for a group of fishermen or anybody that wants a clean room but isn't fussy about amenities. Views from rooms look either towards the bar or the neighbor's back fence. No frills, but a very quick walk to downtown.

Rates

Single: $500 pesos   **currently about $45**
Double: $500 pesos

———— All Prices + 12% tax ————

Promotions: Group and multiple night discounts

Credit Card Acceptance: MasterCard & Visa

Air Conditioning	Satellite / Cable TV	Telephone in Room	Swimming Pool	Jacuzzi	Non Smoking Rooms	Wheelchair Access	Kitchenette	Refrigerator	Microwave	In Room Coffee	Continental Breakfast	On-Site Restaurant	On-Site Store	Lighted Parking
X	X													

Beach	Golf Nearby	Elevator	Dead Bolt Locks	Pets Okay	Meeting Rooms	Balconies	Banquet Facility	Cribs Available	Child Care	In Room Safe	Room Service	Interior Corridors	Exterior Corridors	24 Hr. Security
												X		

The Final Word:

They also rent A.T.V.'s, jet skis and they can take you out fishing as well.

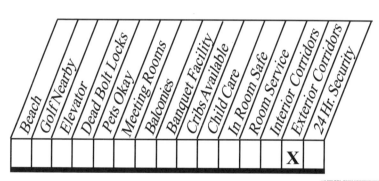

Close to downtown and just minutes to the sea.

8 Blocks

Moderate +

Hacienda Suites

Ave. Salvatierra #152
Loreto, B.C.S. 23880 Mexico

Website:www.haciendasuites.com **E-mail:**reservhaciendasuites@prodigy.net.mx
Phone: 011 52 (613) 135 02 02　**Fax:** 011 52 (613) 135 02 02
Toll free from U.S.A.　(866) 207-8732

Date Opened: 2002
A Word About Location:

　　Arriving from the airport, this property is the first
hotel　as you enter Loreto. It is conveniently across the street
from the bus station and is only a few blocks to the central
plaza and a couple more to the sea.

Facility Description:

　　This all suite hotel opened in 2002 and is a bright
well manicured addition to East Loreto. This is one of the
two nicest non-beach hotels in Loreto and has an on-site
restaurant, two bars and a "child friendly"
swimming pool. For not being in the hotel district, they do a
great job including the services guests need.

Rates

20 Standard Suites 2 Double Beds 770 Pesos currently $70 USD	1 Junior Suite 895 Pesos currently $81 USD	3 Master Suites 957 Pesos currently $87 USD

All Prices + 12% tax

Two children under 12 years old sharing room with their parents free of
charge. Extra persons add $10 USD. Add meals: Full American Plan for
additional $23 USD per person.

Promotions: Check the website

Credit Card Acceptance: MasterCard, Visa, Amex

Air Conditioning	Satellite / Cable TV	Telephone in Room	Swimming Pool	Jacuzzi	Non Smoking Rooms	Wheelchair Access	Kitchenette	Refrigerator	Microwave	In Room Coffee	Continental Breakfast	On-Site Restaurant	On-Site Store	Lighted Parking
X	X		X	X			X			X		X	X	

Beach	Golf Nearby	Elevator	Dead Bolt Locks	Pets Okay	Meeting Rooms	Balconies	Banquet Facility	Cribs Available	Child Care	In Room Safe	Room Service	Interior Corridors	Exterior Corridors	24 Hr. Security
									X	X		X		

The Final Word:

The nicest non-beach moderate class hotel in the city. It is brand new and ready for guests.

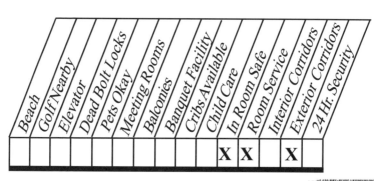

Tennis lessons offered by "Leo the Pro"

Moderate

3 Blocks

The Iguana Inn

located on Benito Juarez between
Madera and Davis Streets

Website: www.iguanainn.com   **E-mail:**iguanainn@yahoo.com
Phone: 011 52 (613) 135 1627

Date Last Remodeled: 2001

A Word About Location:

      The Iguana Inn is one block north of the central plaza and just a block from the sea. It is conveniently located next to the Hotel Posada San Martin and across from the police department.

Facility Description:

      Three spacious bungalows surround a central court-yard. There are VCR's and bikes available along with a small book exchange. The management has over 200 videos to choose from. The BBQ facilities along with a palapa and hammocks make for nice afternoons. The bathrooms have been recently renovated and have nice large showers. In fact, they do a nearly complete remodel on each unit every year to keep them in top shape. The free book exchange boasts a couple hundred books.

Rates

Three bungalows ranging from 400-450 pesos per
night. Currently $ 36-40 USD
including tax

Promotions: Check website.

Credit Card Acceptance: None

Air Conditioning	Satellite / Cable TV	Telephone in Room	Swimming Pool	Jacuzzi	Non Smoking Rooms	Wheelchair Access	Kitchenette	Refrigerator	Microwave	In Room Coffee	Continental Breakfast	On-Site Restaurant	On-Site Store	Lighted Parking
X								X	X	X				X

Beach	Golf Nearby	Elevator	Dead Bolt Locks	Pets Okay	Meeting Rooms	Balconies	Banquet Facility	Cribs Available	Child Care	In Room Safe	Room Service	Interior Corridors	Exterior Corridors	24 Hr. Security
												X	X	

The Final Word:

Book all three rooms and it's like your own house.

Nice Bathrooms

Budget

Hotel Junipero

Ave. Hidalgo #1 s/n Loreto,
B.C.S. 23880 Mexico

Phone: 011 52 (613) 135 0122 **Fax:** 011 52 (613) 135 0028

A Word About Location:

The Hotel Junipero is close to everything downtown. One block from the central plaza and two blocks from the Sea of Cortez. It is across the street from the Hotel Plaza Loreto.

Facility Description:

This downtown hotel has 24 rooms and part of its sign is falling down, but it is right across the street from the city's historical mission. The lobby has coffee and a water cooler. There is also a T.V. in the lobby that apparently sometimes works in case you get excited about watching a show with the front desk guy. 12 of the rooms have a refrigerator and in the room we checked it was actually keeping cold. It is not the Ritz, but for people on a tight budget you could do a lot worse.

Rates

Single	Double	Triple
$30 USD	$36 USD	$40USD

All Prices + 12% tax

Promotions: None

Credit Card Acceptance: None

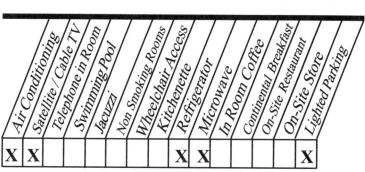

Air Conditioning	Satellite / Cable TV	Telephone in Room	Swimming Pool	Jacuzzi	Non Smoking Rooms	Wheelchair Access	Kitchenette	Refrigerator	Microwave	In Room Coffee	Continental Breakfast	On-Site Restaurant	On-Site Store	Lighted Parking
X	X						X	X						X

Beach	Golf Nearby	Elevator	Dead Bolt Locks	Pets Okay	Meeting Rooms	Balconies	Banquet Facility	Cribs Available	Child Care	In Room Safe	Room Service	Interior Corridors	Exterior Corridors	24 Hr. Security
					X							X	X	

The Final Word:

The closest you can stay to
Our Lady of Loreto Mission.

Location
Location
Location

9 Blocks

Hotel La Pinta

Prolongacion Fco. J. Madero
Loreto, B.C.S. 23880 Mexico

Beachfront property

Website: www.lapintahotels.com **E-mail** lapintaloreto@prodigy.net.mx
Phone: 011 52 (613) 5 00 25   **Fax:** 011 52 (613) 135 00 26
Phone Toll Free from US and Can. (800) 800-9632

Date Opened and Last Remodeled: Opened in 1972
remodeled in 1997.

A Word About Location:

At the north end of the malecon, this property is just over a kilometer from the central plaza, but it is right on the Sea of Cortez and just a short walk to the malecon.

Facility Description:

48 rooms that are right on the beach. This hotel is clean, air conditioned and some rooms include fireplaces. The on-site restaurant serves good Mexican food and a peek into the kitchen will reveal about half a dozen Mexican ladies hustling around in white preparing your meals. Considered a motor inn, but you get a nice clean room with a great view. There is a nice pool with a bar close by as well as a small game room.

Rates		
Standard Hacienda	Villa	extra person
$79 USD	$100 USD	$15 USD

All Prices + 12% tax

Promotions: check website

Credit Card Acceptance: MasterCard, Visa, Amex

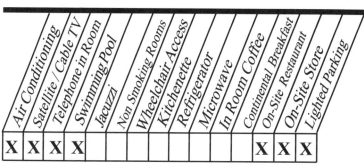

Air Conditioning	Satellite / Cable TV	Telephone in Room	Swimming Pool	Jacuzzi	Non Smoking Rooms	Wheelchair Access	Kitchenette	Refrigerator	Microwave	In Room Coffee	Continental Breakfast	On-Site Restaurant	On-Site Store	Lighted Parking
X	X	X	X								X	X	X	

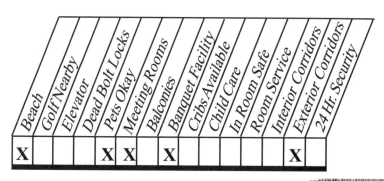

Beach	Golf Nearby	Elevator	Dead Bolt Locks	Pets Okay	Meeting Rooms	Balconies	Banquet Facility	Cribs Available	Child Care	In Room Safe	Room Service	Interior Corridors	Exterior Corridors	24 Hr. Security
X				X	X		X				X			

The Final Word:

Check later: management has plans for an R.V. park as well. The ice cream freezer in the lobby featuring 22 different novelty frozen treats is a good thing.

Ask the front desk for wood for your fireplace

1.1 kilometers

Beachfront property

Loreto Playa

APDO Postal 127 Loreto,
B.C.S. 23880 México

Website:www.loretaplaya.com **Email:** loretoplaya@prodigy.net.mx
Phone:011 52 (613) 135 1129 **Fax:** 011 52 (613) 135 1129

Date Built: 1996
A Word About Location:

It is eight blocks from the central plaza on the beach just 200 meters north of the Hotel La Pinta. It is a block or so beyond the end of the paved road but given the terrain and the architecture employed in its construction, the location ends up being great.

Facility Description:

Built with couples in mind, this bed and breakfast offers a beautiful facility and a high level of service. Starting at the top you enjoy a 360 degree view with a two level porch that offers views of the Sea of Cortez and the Sierra Gigante mountains. Stepping inside you find an amazing master bedroom with a canopy bed and romantic atmosphere. The house is tastefully decorated and features local and international works of art. A full breakfast is served and is included in the price. There are four rooms and they do not accept walk-ins.

Rates

$135 USD which
includes tax and
breakfast.

Reservations needed

Promotions: check website

Credit Card Acceptance: via paypal

Air Conditioning	Satellite / Cable TV	Telephone in Room	Swimming Pool	Jacuzzi	Non Smoking Rooms	Wheelchair Access	Kitchenette	Refrigerator	Microwave	In Room Coffee	Continental Breakfast	On-Site Restaurant	On-Site Store	Lighted Parking
X	X						X	X	X					

Beach	Golf Nearby	Elevator	Dead Bolt Locks	Pets Okay	Meeting Rooms	Balconies	Banquet Facility	Cribs Available	Child Care	In Room Safe	Room Service	Interior Corridors	Exterior Corridors	24 Hr. Security
X					X									

The Final Word:

The proprietors didn't stop with providing a great facility. They also have ocean kayaks and mountain bikes for use by the guests free of charge.

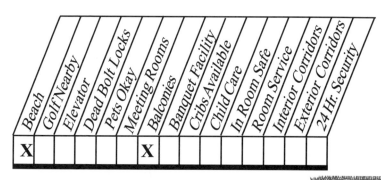

Marine life up close on the beach

3 Blocks

Budget

El Moro Motel
& R.V. Park
Rosendo Robles No. 8 Loreto,
B.C.S. 23880 Mexico

Phone: 011 52 (613) 135 0542   **Fax:** 011 52 (613) 135 0788

A Word About Location:

One block from the sea down one of the streets that isn't yet paved. You do have to hike a block or more for food or entertainment even though you are just two blocks from the central plaza.

Facility Description:

Eight rooms in this Motel that has a giant fenced parking area for your car, boat or R.V. Nice bright doors lead you into a pretty comfortable room that you wouldn't expect from seeing the outside. The bathrooms are small but clean. Outside there are two bathrooms with showers for those using the R.V. park. They also offer $3.00 USD laundry service. Check at the front desk.

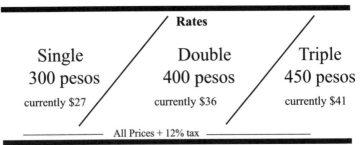

Rates

Single	Double	Triple
300 pesos	400 pesos	450 pesos
currently $27	currently $36	currently $41

All Prices + 12% tax

R.V. Park rates - 1 Day 130 Pesos   Stay one week get one day free.   1 Month 2500 Pesos

Credit Card Acceptance: None

Air Conditioning	Satellite / Cable TV	Telephone in Room	Swimming Pool	Jacuzzi	Non Smoking Rooms	Wheelchair Access	Kitchenette	Refrigerator	Microwave	In Room Coffee	Continental Breakfast	On-Site Restaurant	On-Site Store	Lighted Parking
X	X								X					X

Beach	Golf Nearby	Elevator	Dead Bolt Locks	Pets Okay	Meeting Rooms	Balconies	Banquet Facility	Cribs Available	Child Care	In Room Safe	Room Service	Interior Corridors	Exterior Corridors	24 Hr. Security
													X	X

The Final Word:

      If you need a lot of room for an R.V. or a boat they have it, and only two blocks from the boat launch.

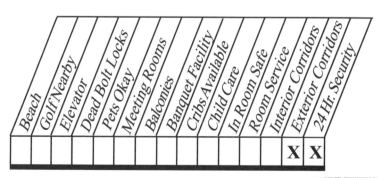

Amazing crustacean collection on a shelf in front office

6 Blocks

Beachfront property

Hotel Oasis

Calle Baja California y Lopez
Mateos s/n PO Box 17 Loreto,
B.C.S. 23880 Mexico

Website: www.hoteloasis.com   **E-mail** loretooasis@prodigy.net.mx
Phone: 011 52 (613) 135 0211   **Fax:** 011 52 (613) 135 0795
Phone Toll Free from US: (800) 497-3923

A Word About Location:

The Hotel Oasis is at the south end of the malecon. It is just four blocks from the central plaza and is one of the few properties in Loreto that has it's own beach access.

Facility Description:

39 rooms including 4 suites in this hotel make it a good bet for groups or couples wanting to be on the beach while keeping to a budget. The standard rooms are simple but clean. Moving up to a suite brings not only a larger room but also a newly remodeled living area including new furniture. The restaurant is open from 6 am until 9:30 pm. The bar is open from 1 pm until 10:30pm or later if there is a crowd. They also have their own fishing boats available for charter.

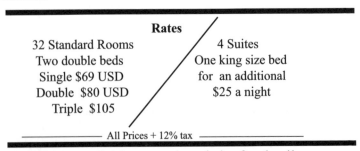

Rates

32 Standard Rooms	4 Suites
Two double beds	One king size bed
Single $69 USD	for an additional
Double $80 USD	$25 a night
Triple $105	

All Prices + 12% tax

Meal Plans available; consult website for details
Promotions: Special packages that include fishing

Credit Card Acceptance: MasterCard and Visa

Air Conditioning	Satellite / Cable TV	Telephone in Room	Swimming Pool	Jacuzzi	Non Smoking Rooms	Wheelchair Access	Kitchenette	Refrigerator	Microwave	In Room Coffee	Continental Breakfast	On-Site Restaurant	On-Site Store	Lighted Parking
X	X	X	X						X		X			X

Beach	Golf Nearby	Elevator	Dead Bolt Locks	Pets Okay	Meeting Rooms	Balconies	Banquet Facility	Cribs Available	Child Care	In Room Safe	Room Service	Interior Corridors	Exterior Corridors	24 Hr. Security
X			X	X									X	X

The Final Word:

If you have a few extra bucks then upgrade to a suite. It is a big difference in comfort. Internet available in lobby $3 USD for 30 min. or $5 USD for 60min.

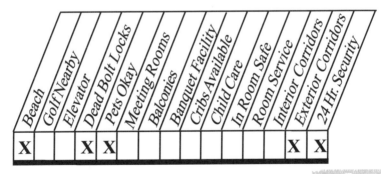

Satellite Television available from the lobby by request

10 Kilometers

Moderate

Olive Tree Villas

Nopolo, 23880
Loreto, B.C.S.Mexico

Website: www.olivetreevillas.com **E-mail:**info@olivetreevillas.com
Phone: 011 52 (613) 133 02 75   **Fax:** 011 52 (613) 133 02 32

A Word About Location:

Olive Tree Villas are in Nopolo not far from the Camino Real and the golf course. It is 5 kilometers south of the airport and 10 kilometers south of the central plaza in Loreto. It is three blocks to the beach and the local tennis club is nearby as well. Located in an area without much to do without a car, the coming years promise more development nearby.

Facility Description:.

Just four suites make up the Olive Tree Villas, but for a relaxing retreat not teeming with neighbors this property features a nice pool, attractively furnished rooms and beautiful sunsets. There is a restaurant across the street, as well as a good sized market.

Rates		
Suite 1	Suite 2	Suite 3 or 4
$145 USD a night	$120 USD a night	$65 USD a night
3 Bedrooms	2 Bedrooms	
3 Baths / Kitchen	2 Baths / Kitchen	1 Bedroom / 1 bath
Entertainment Room	Entertainment Room	Kitchen / Ent. Room

All Prices + 12% tax

Promotions: None

Credit Card Acceptance: None

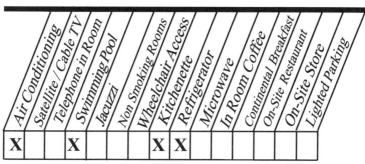

Air Conditioning	Satellite / Cable TV	Telephone in Room	Swimming Pool	Jacuzzi	Non Smoking Rooms	Wheelchair Access	Kitchenette	Refrigerator	Microwave	In Room Coffee	Continental Breakfast	On-Site Restaurant	On-Site Store	Lighted Parking
X		X				X	X							

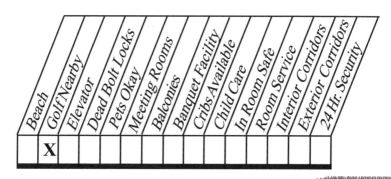

Beach	Golf Nearby	Elevator	Dead Bolt Locks	Pets Okay	Meeting Rooms	Balconies	Banquet Facility	Cribs Available	Child Care	In Room Safe	Room Service	Interior Corridors	Exterior Corridors	24 Hr. Security
	X													

The Final Word:

It is pretty far from downtown but you have a small grocery store nearby as well as tennis, golf and beach access nearby.

The tennis club up the street is still like new.

6 Blocks

Ultra-Budget

Hotel Palmas Altas

Nicolas Bravo s/n El Baja y Moro
Loreto, B.C.S. 23880 Mexico

Website: www.hotelpalmasaltas.com
Phone: 011 52 (613) 135 13 53

A Word About Location:

Five or six blocks to the central plaza and about a block and a half from the Sea of Cortez. It sits down a dirt road south of the city center.

Facility Description:

24 rooms in this hotel that should remind the guest of staying in a mobile home from the early seventies. The rooms have two twin beds It seems to be holding together well and although the pool is small, it is nice and features an aerobics trampoline for a diving board. It actually isn't a bad hotel and has its own charm but not really what you might expect. If you are looking for something like home then this isn't it, but it is affordable and out of the way. Another choice for fisherman or tourist on a tight budget.

Rates		
Room	Suite	Apartment
Single 220 Pesos	450 Pesos	500 Pesos
Dbl. 275 Pesos		
$ 20-25	currently $41	currently $45

All Prices + 12% tax

Promotions: none

Credit Card Acceptance: MasterCard, Visa

Air Conditioning	Satellite / Cable TV	Telephone in Room	Swimming Pool	Jacuzzi	Non Smoking Rooms	Wheelchair Access	Kitchenette	Refrigerator	Microwave	In Room Coffee	Continental Breakfast	On-Site Restaurant	On-Site Store	Lighted Parking
X	X		X	X									X	

Beach	Golf Nearby	Elevator	Dead Bolt Locks	Pets Okay	Meeting Rooms	Balconies	Banquet Facility	Cribs Available	Child Care	In Room Safe	Room Service	Interior Corridors	Exterior Corridors	24 Hr. Security
											X			

The Final Word:

> Well, it is yellow and has fenced parking.

Great place to write a retro space alien movie

2 Blocks

Budget +

Hotel Plaza Loreto

Paseo Hidalgo No. 2 Loreto
B.C.S. 23880 Mexico

Website: www.loreto.com/plazaloreto
E-mail: hotelplazaloreto@prodigy.net.mx
Phone: 01 52 (613) 135 0280   **Fax:** 011 52 (613) 135 0855

A Word About Location:

The hotel is one long block from the sea and is right in the middle of the historic downtown center, only about a block from the central plaza.

Facility Description:

This is an older property but it is still pretty well maintained. There are 24 rooms with bedding and furniture that are attractive and new. An upstairs patio with a small table makes for a relaxing spot to play games or just lounge in the evenings. In the same building there is a pharmacy, a travel agency and a laundry facility. For downtown living it is a good choice, for an inexpensive, non-beach hotel.

Rates		
September- November		December- August
Single $30 USD		Single $39
Double $35 USD		Double $42
Triple $40 USD		Triple $47
All Prices + 12% tax		

Promotions: The sign out front advertises a special but call or check on the internet if you don't happen to be out in front of the hotel.

Credit Card Acceptance: MasterCard, Visa

Air Conditioning	Satellite / Cable TV	Telephone in Room	Swimming Pool	Jacuzzi	Non Smoking Rooms	Wheelchair Access	Kitchenette	Refrigerator	Microwave	In Room Coffee	Continental Breakfast	On-Site Restaurant	On-Site Store	Lighted Parking
X	X												X	

Beach	Golf Nearby	Elevator	Dead Bolt Locks	Pets Okay	Meeting Rooms	Balconies	Banquet Facility	Cribs Available	Child Care	In Room Safe	Room Service	Interior Corridors	Exterior Corridors	24 Hr. Security
			X										X	X

The Final Word:

    The noise from the street can get loud so try for a room towards the back. For the price, this hotel is a good bet.

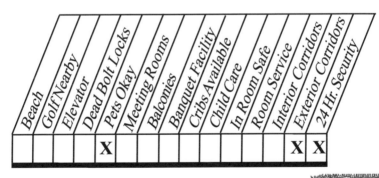

Super Location Fair Prices

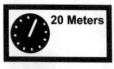

Deluxe +

Hotel Posada
de las Flores
Salvatierra esq. Madero Col. Centro
Loreto, B.C.S. 23880 Mexico

Website: www.posadadelasflores.com **E-mail:** hotel@posadadelasflores.com
Phone: 011 52 (613) 135 1162   **Fax:** 011 52 (613) 135 1099

Date Built: 1999

A Word About Location:

Right in the middle of downtown Loreto across the street from the central plaza, this hotel is close to shopping, the sea, nightlife and points of historical interest.

Facility Description:

The nicest non-beach hotel in Loreto, this "boutique" hotel has 15 units. 10 standard rooms and 5 junior suites. Each standard room includes a 27" TV, telephone, safety deposit box and a hair dryer. Upgrade to a junior suite and find a minibar, bathrobes and a king sized bed. Call the front desk for complimentary video movies. They feature 2 restaurants, one of which serves Italian and Mexican food in a rooftop garden environment. The other is an Italian restaurant that is open during the high season. Just up and over from the restaurant is a rooftop pool that allows swimmers to look through the bottom into the lobby below.

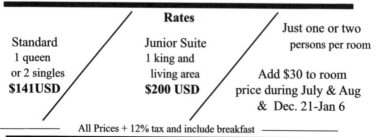

Rates

Standard	Junior Suite	Just one or two persons per room
1 queen or 2 singles	1 king and living area	Add $30 to room price during July & Aug & Dec. 21-Jan 6
$141USD	**$200 USD**	

All Prices + 12% tax and include breakfast

Promotions: check website

Credit Card Acceptance: MasterCard, Visa

Air Conditioning	Satellite / Cable TV	Telephone in Room	Swimming Pool	Jacuzzi	Non Smoking Rooms	Wheelchair Access	Kitchenette	Refrigerator	Microwave	In Room Coffee	Continental Breakfast	On-Site Restaurant	On-Site Store	Lighted Parking
X	X	X	X				X		X					

Beach	Golf Nearby	Elevator	Dead Bolt Locks	Pets Okay	Meeting Rooms	Balconies	Banquet Facility	Cribs Available	Child Care	In Room Safe	Room Service	Interior Corridors	Exterior Corridors	24 Hr. Security
									X	X	X			

The Final Word:

The coffee service brought to your room starts the royal treatment guests receive every day at Posada de la Flores.

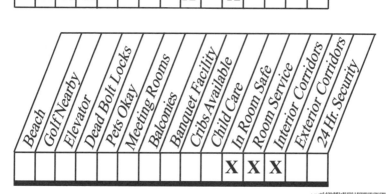

Best view in Loreto from atop the Hotel

Hotel Quinta
San Francisco

Budget +

Blvd. Adolfo Lopez Mateos Entre. Ave Juarez y Agua Dulce, Loreto, B.C.S. 23880 Mexico

E-mail: hotelquintasanfrancisco@prodgiy.net.mx
Phone: 011 52 (613) 135 10 88   **Fax:** 011 52 (613) 5 10 89

Date Last Remodeled: 2001
A Word About Location:

This hotel is on the street facing the Sea of Cortez and the malecon. Just three blocks from the central plaza. There are some restaurants within a block or two.

Facility Description:

More of a guest house than hotel, this property has 6 guest quarters. Some with 2 double beds and some with 1 double and 1 single. The rooms are clean and well maintained. What sets it apart is its great location looking right out over the sea. It is the perfect place to set out on a moon lit walk along the malecon. The year 2001 remodel took the property into its present form. Before that it had been a restaurant for many years. They will be installing cable television soon.

Rates

1 - 3 People $39 USD
includes tax

Promotions: Buy 6 days and get 1 free.

Credit Card Acceptance: None

Air Conditioning	Satellite / Cable TV	Telephone in Room	Swimming Pool	Jacuzzi	Non Smoking Rooms	Wheelchair Access	Kitchenette	Refrigerator	Microwave	In Room Coffee	Continental Breakfast	On-Site Restaurant	On-Site Store	Lighted Parking
X				X										

Beach	Golf Nearby	Elevator	Dead Bolt Locks	Pets Okay	Meeting Rooms	Balconies	Banquet Facility	Cribs Available	Child Care	In Room Safe	Room Service	Interior Corridors	Exterior Corridors	24 Hr. Security
													X	

The Final Word: The owner keeps these rooms immaculate. Partiers should book elsewhere. They are looking for guests who know how to respect others property and are interested in seeing the sights and enjoying the property for relaxation.

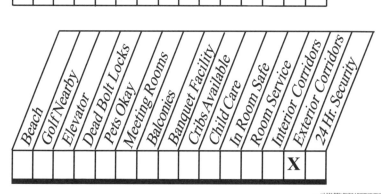

Great Location to start a moonlit stroll

SuKasa Bungalows

4 Blocks

Moderate

Blvd. Lopez Mateo y Calle
Fernando Jordan Loreto,
B.C.S. 23880 Mexico

Website:www.sukasa@loretoweb.com.mx **E-mail:** sukasa@prodigy.net.mx
Phone: 011 52 (613) 135 0490   **Fax:** 011 52 (613) 135 0490

Date Last Remodeled: 1998

A Word About Location:

SuKasa Bungalows are across from the malecon and about three blocks south of the Hotel Quinta San Francisco. Close to restaurants and just two blocks from the central plaza.

Facility Description:

These bungalows each have one bedroom, a living room, dining and kitchen areas. Big bathrooms and good air conditioning make these a comfortable choice. There is a large shared terrace with lounge chairs and a hammock or two. 2 pm check-out is a plus, but they do ask that guests reduce noise after 10 pm.   The lighted parking is on the street.

Rates

By the Day	By the Week	By the Month
$65 USD	$440 USD	$1500 USD

All Prices + 12% tax

Promotions: Check the website

Credit Card Acceptance: MasterCard, Visa

Air Conditioning	Satellite / Cable TV	Telephone in Room	Swimming Pool	Jacuzzi	Non Smoking Rooms	Wheelchair Access	Kitchenette	Refrigerator	Microwave	In Room Coffee	Continental Breakfast	On-Site Restaurant	On-Site Store	Lighted Parking
X							X	X	X				X	

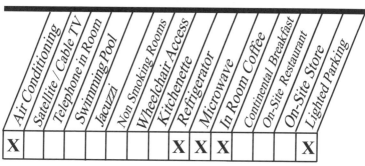

Beach	Golf Nearby	Elevator	Dead Bolt Locks	Pets Okay	Meeting Rooms	Balconies	Banquet Facility	Cribs Available	Child Care	In Room Safe	Room Service	Interior Corridors	Exterior Corridors	24 Hr. Security
														X

The Final Word:

Great location for people who want to be right on the sea.   Management is responsive and ready to help you have a great trip to Loreto.

Their Motto is mi casa es SuKasa

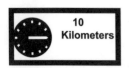

Beachfront property

Whales Inn

Blvd Mision de Loreto s/n.
Col. Loreto Nopolo,
Loreto, B.C.S. 23880 Mexico

Website: www.whalesinnloreto.com
Phone: 011 52 (613) 133 0700
Reservations Toll Free from U.S. : 1-800-353-4988

formerly Solare Resort

A Word About Location:

The Whales Inn is situated in Nopolo, across the street from the Loreto Tennis Center. It is a short walk to the golf course and is 10 km from downtown Loreto or about a 10 minute taxi ride. It is also adjacent to the Villages of Loreto Bay development.

Facility Description:

This hotel has lots of room to relax in the sun. Most of the rooms are on the smaller side but still clean. The pool area and beach offer ample room to lay in the sun. There are two restaurants and a poolside snack shack which offers hot food and drinks. The rooms are outfitted with color TV's, air conditioning and many have a great view of the Sea of Cortez. Upper floor rooms have balconies and first floor have garden patios.   There is a stage near the pool for entertainment.

Rates

All inclusive $170 Single
$115 per person / Double Occupancy
extra persons $82.50

All Prices + 12% tax

Promotions: Contact hotel. In Jan 2005 $85 pp all inclusive

Credit Card Acceptance: MasterCard, Visa

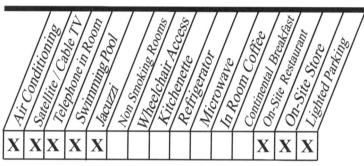

Air Conditioning	Satellite / Cable TV	Telephone in Room	Swimming Pool	Jacuzzi	Non Smoking Rooms	Wheelchair Access	Kitchenette	Refrigerator	Microwave	In Room Coffee	Continental Breakfast	On-Site Restaurant	On-Site Store	Lighted Parking
X	X	X	X	X							X	X	X	

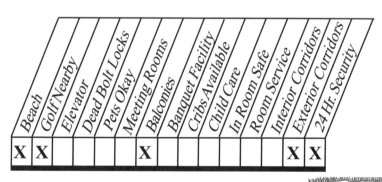

Beach	Golf Nearby	Elevator	Dead Bolt Locks	Pets Okay	Meeting Rooms	Balconies	Banquet Facility	Cribs Available	Child Care	In Room Safe	Room Service	Interior Corridors	Exterior Corridors	24 Hr. Security
X	X				X								X	X

The Final Word:

This hotel has undergone three incarnations in the last years including a time as an adults only resort. The bank is managing it as of the beginning of 2005 and is looking for a buyer. Keep watch for new owners and possibly a new name.

Lots of Potential but waiting for an owner to give it some TLC

Dining

Restaurants

El Canipole: Tel: 011 52 (613) 135 1886

Pino Suarez and Magdalena de Kino   Mexican

Breakfast, Lunch, Dinner Daily   from 8am-11pm except on
Sunday which is from 2pm - 8pm

They have a guest book full of compliments from past guests
including one from us. The soft music and the off the main
street location add to the romantic atmosphere.

Their motto is, "Art in food, in the oldest Restaurant in Loreto."
     "Arte en comida en la lugar mas antigua de Loreto"

Cesars Taco y Taco

Corner of Miguel Hidalgo y Cologio.   Tacos

It is a roadside taco stand with sit down dining and a few
extra menu items.

Chile Willie Restaurant:

(on the north end of the Malecon)

Fresh Seafood / Mexican Food

Hours: closed and currently undergoing extensive remodeling.
Hopefully it will be open again when you arrive. It is right on
the beach. You can't eat any closer to the sea off of a boat.

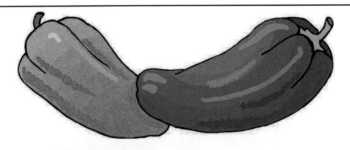

Restaurants

La Cazuelas   Tel: 011 52 (613) 135 0025

Located at La Pinta Hotel   Mexican,Seafood

Breakfast, Lunch, Dinner   Hours 6am - 10 pm 7 days.

Guaycura: Tel: 011 52 (613) 133 0010

 Located at the Camino Real

Breakfast and Dinner

Buffet style restaurant featuring Mexican and international entrees.

The Lobster Trap   Tel: 011 52 (613) 135 0027

Corner of Calle Indepencia y Benito Juarez Juarez

Closed Tuesdays   Seafood / Bar

A great building and great atmosphere for getting together with friends to eat and drink in an atmosphere one would expect to find when going to Mexico to drink some tequila or beer.

Restaurants

Rancho Viejo

Located at the Hacienda Suites.   Mexican

Small, but nice dining room in this brand new restaurant and hotel.

Hours 6:30am - 10pm

Rigas Tacos: Tacos

Taco stand built into front of house on main drag just across from Hotel Plaza Loreto. The T.V. and the salsa selection at this taco stand make it a convenient late night option.

The Roof Garden: 011 52 (613) 135 1162

Located at the Hotel Posada de las Flores   Mexican

Dinner

Beautiful views of the Sea of Cortez and the Sierra Gigante Moutains.

Restaurants

Salvatierra: 011 52 (613) 133 0010

Located at the Camino Real   Italian / Mexican

Breakfast / Lunch / Dinner   when not open the Guaycura
will be open.

They have a full menu including very good seafood, and
offer Argentine style steaks as a specialty.

Taqueria "La Reyna"

Paseo Hidalgo y Pino Suarez   Tacos

Watch them cook your tacos at this street side grill

El Taste La Casa del Rib Eye   011 52 (613) 135 1489

Located on Benito Juarez & Zapata   Mexican / Seafood

Fantastic staff, great atmosphere and the steaks were big
enough for 2 people. The meal came with a baked potato
and vegetables. Great for groups or couples and has a full
bar.

Places to See

Places to See

Islands off of Loreto:

There are several islands in the Sea of Cortez off of Loreto that you can visit and explore. Some of which are able to be reached by ocean kayak and many enjoy camping on the beautiful beaches of these islands. It is requested that you do not bring any animals with you onto the islands. The five closest islands are:

Coronado: At 2.5 kilometers from Loreto this island is home to sea lion colonies and beautiful water for diving.

Carmen: 13 kilometers out, this large island is known for its lovely beaches and the cliffs on the eastern shore that rise 100 feet above the sea.

Danzante: About 23 kilometers south of Loreto this island has many coves and rock formations. One cove of note is Honeymoon Cove which has a great beach and hosts many kayakers throughout the year.

Monserrat: This island has many coves and is the destination for many night time lobster hunting expeditions. The island has yellow sandstone cliffs and lots of terrain for hiking. There are some rock outcroppings that make for a good diving spot.

Santa Catalina: Home to unique flora and fauna and a favorite of scientists and those who love nature.

Places to See

Puerto Escondido:

This is a very well protected anchorage that is eventually going to include a hotel, restaurants and boating services. For now there is a half-built hotel that does not seem as though it will be finished anytime soon and a pier that allows for fairly large boats to tie up. Water is available but not much more without going to the nearby trailer park or Loreto. About a half mile up the road, the El Tripui Trailer Park has a restaurant and small store. The restaurant is open from 1:30pm until 9pm and there is also internet access for those who do not like to be out of touch.

From Loreto you travel about 24 kilometers south on the transpeninsular highway and turn left at the sign.

On the way to Puerto Escondido on the highway about 5 kilometers south of Nopolo is a beachside restaurant named Vista al Mar. It is right on the beach and offers budget outdoor dining.

Desert Garden Oasis:

A destination for hikers, mountain bikes or burro rides. This area is home to varied terrain and some working ranches. Scheduled tours are available with guides that tell you about the history of the area and lead you through hidden canyons and to vistas within the Sierra Gigante.

The Practicals

<u>Phone / Internet / Mail / Money Transfer / Pharmacy / Medical Problems / Accessibility Issues / Car Rentals / Real Estate Investment</u>

Phone Service

Dial Direct to the U.S.A. - 001 + area code + seven digit number.

Dial Direct to other countries. - 00 + country code + area code + number.

When calling using coins you dial the number first and then the operator tells you how much to deposit.

A better option is using prepaid phone cards that are available at most stores, pharmacies and gift shops. Put the card in the slot and then dial out direct.

Another good option is to use your calling card from home. Many include access numbers to call without using coins from other countries. You are connected to an English speaking operator or are allowed to use the English speaking automated system just as if you were at home.

For M.C. I. Worldcom Cards
dial 01 - 800 - 674 - 7000   from Telmex phones

For A.T.T. Cards
dial 01 - 800 - 288 - 2872 or
001 800 462 4240

For Sprint Cards
dial 001- 800 - 877 - 8000   from Ladatel phones

The pay phones often encourage you to dial direct using a major credit card. These calls are usually much more expensive than one of the other options discussed.

Local payphones in Loreto are Telmex. Phone cards can be purchased at many local stores. When calling collect, a service charge of 30% is added to the price of the call. Local payphone calls cost 2.5 pesos per minute and international calls cost 5 pesos per minute

<u>Getting Cash</u>

Apparently there is only one cash machine in Loreto. It is in the bank across the street from the central plaza. (Bancomer) The sign outside says caja automatica and it is available 24 hours a day.

Most hotels will also exchange money but automatic teller machines generally offer better rates. Also note that the cash machine dispenses only Pesos.

Internet Access

Remember that the keyboards in Mexico are a bit different, to accomodate the additional symbols and punctuation. For example on some keyboards it is necessary to hold down the alt key and then press 6 on the number pad then 4 to get the @ sign to appear. If it isn't like home then ask an employee for help.

Our number one choice for internet access in Loreto is **Ram 64**, a internet cafe on Calle Benito Juarez just about four and a half blocks from the central plaza. They cater to locals but seem to be the most knowledgeable in case you need assistance. They have six computers all at least 1.1 gigahertz, but the connections are the usual Mexican 56K.

Prices:
Internet usage: 1-20 minutes   3 pesos
                21-40 minutes   6 pesos
                41-60 minutes   9 pesos

Black & White Print   2 pesos
Blank CD's $15 pesos   Color Print - text   3 pesos
(Student Discount 10%)   ask about photos
Business Hours:
        Monday-Friday 10 am - 2 pm & 4 pm-10 pm
        Saturday is the same except they close at 9 pm.

If you are waiting for someone to check their email, the aerobics studio that shares the building makes for an interesting diversion.

Your next option is the **Caseta Soledad,** an internet cafe with seven computers. It is on the main drag that comes into town from the airport. It is on Calle Salvatierra about two blocks from the bus station and about six blocks from the central plaza in the other direction. 20 pesos / hour

---

Third on our list is the **Compu - Mas.com** computer and sign shop. It is air-conditioned and they also repair computers and make signs. Located a block north of Hacienda Suites.

Hours: Monday - Saturday 9am - 1pm 4pm - 8:30pm

Finally we have (**.Com**) (right next to the Cafe Ole)

Phone / Fax 135 1847 Calle Francisco Madero #16

This internet cafe is only 50 meters away from the central plaza and has four internet stations. They also offer fax services and long distance phone calls.

Internet time goes for 20 pesos / hour. The fax service seems to be a bargain though with the cost being the same even if you are sending back to America. 1or 2 pages will run you 15 pesos but send 5-7 and it is only 40 pesos.

Mail

The Post office is just off of Salvatierra on Calle Ignacio Allende near the Red Cross building. It is the only post office in Loreto. Locals have warned that sometimes mail service to and from the states can take quite a while.

Hours of operation: Monday - Fri   8am - 3p

Closed Saturday & Sunday

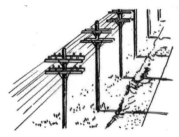

Money Transfer

Next door to the post office is the local telegraph office. They also handle money transfer and can send a fax or place a long distance call for you.

Hours of operation: Monday - Friday 8am - 2pm
                                Saturday 8am - 11am
                                Closed Sunday

Visa Requirements

Tourist or those staying for less than 180 days at a time just need a standard tourist visa. Make sure that the immigration officer knows how long you will be staying in Mexico. Those wishing to stay for more than 180 days will need to apply for a different kind of visa. There are several different visas, so make sure you are looking at the one that best suits your needs. Generally they need to be renewed every year but some allow for permanent immigration status after five years.

Medical Problems

Larger population centers in Mexico are advancing fairly rapidly in the medical field. Loreto is unique in that even though it is relatively small it has many of these same advances. If you do need a doctor, they do have a couple of hospitals, one of which has been receiving upgrades through a sister city relationship with Hermosa Beach, California.

Nice hotels can help you arrange medical care but, if you find yourself on your own , **call the Paramedics at 135 1566.** They have ambulances to retrieve you.

Loreto has two hospitals. The Centro de Salud is the hospital for everyone and the beneficiary of the equipment from California. They have ten beds and a full operating room. **135 0039.**   The ISSTE Hospital is for those with Mexican insurance but will accept emergency patients. Most locals we have talked with recommend the Centro de Salud. Secondary to the paramedics you can **call the Red Cross at 135 1111.**

If you want to return to the United States for medical treatment and you can't wait until the next scheduled flight out, there are air ambulance companies that can fly you north for treatment. The advantage of going this route is that you have the advantage of having trained medical workers on hand as you travel for more extensive treatment. There are many such companies so you should check the internet before you depart for Mexico.

Pharmacies

Farmacia de las Californias: 135 0341

This pharmacy is located next to the El Pescador Supermarket.

Hours: 7 days a week   8am-10pm

Farmacia Flores: 135 0321

This pharmacy is on the corner of Ave. Salvatierra and Ave. Luis Donolo Calusio.

Hours: 7 days a week   8am-10pm

Farmacia del Rosario #1:   135 0670

This pharmacy is located on the corner of Calle Independencia and Calle B. Juarez.

Hours: 7 days a week   8am-10pm

Farmacia del Rosario #2:   135 0719

This pharmacy is located across from the El Pescador Supermarket

Hours: 7 days a week   8am-10pm

Real Estate Investment:

You can move to Mexico or keep a holiday house south of the border. If your goal is to move within 50 kilometers of the coast or 100 kilometers from the border it takes some additional paperwork to ensure that your ownership will be respected.

This paper work is called a Fideicomiso and is actually a bank trust. The property is placed in the name of the purchaser and is held in trust by a bank. The bank administers the property under the direction of the owner. The owner / beneficiary of the trust enjoys normal property rights including the right to build, rent out and to sell the property. The property is also able to be passed on in an estate. These trusts are valid for up to 50 years and are able to be renewed The paper work for these transactions is extensive so make sure that you deal with a reputable notary who has a track record in this field. Mexican law says that the trust can be renewed indefinitely within the terms established by law. The cost can be under $2000 USD.

The Villages of Loreto Bay:

Just a few kilometers south of Loreto, a new development is already being built and is of a scale seldom seen anywhere. Marketed as a pedestrian friendly community, they offer custom built homes in a variety of designs and floorplans. They have frequent informational meetings in the United States and Canada as well as hosting trips to Loreto. Their partnership with Alaska Airlines to bring tourists to Loreto will certainly bring growth to the area. Imagine having the opportunity to buy property in Cabo twenty years ago knowing what they would be worth today. That, along with an environmentally friendly and exclusive address is drawing people to purchase both investment property and second homes in Loreto Bay.

The Villages of Loreto Bay continued:

The laws concerning property ownership have evolved over the last years and are now very buyer friendly. Title insurance is available for home purchases in this development.

<u>Accessibility Issues</u>

The city planners put extra effort into making this city wheelchair accessible. It seems that most street intersections in the shopping district have wide ramps to get up on the sidewalks. Trouble is that apparently nobody told them that the cobblestone and brick streets that lead up to the ramps are not really wheelchair friendly. There are places to go but it isn't perfect by any means.

Most properties have barriers in the form of stairs or random things to step over. Some properties are almost totally accessible, but double check the websites first or email ahead to ask. As tourism grows in Loreto the need to design hotels and facilities with better access will eventually catch up but for now it will require a bit more work if you use mobility assistance devices.

Car Rentals:

Budget Car Rental:

Paseo Hidalgo y Malecon
Also located at Hotel La Pinta

Tel:	011 52 (613) 135 1090
Toll Free:	1-800-472-3325
e-mail:	budgetloreto@prodigy.net.mx
website:	www.budget.com.mx

Rodolfo Palacios - Manager

Prices start at about $53 a day for a small car but if you plan on driving to San Javier you might want to upgrade to a jeep which was $76 a day when we checked. Those prices include tax, surcharges, and unlimited mileage. Both companies seemed pretty similar in cost.

Hertz Car Rental:

Av. Salvatierra y Calle Romanita

Tel:	011 52 (613) 135 0800
Fax:	011 52 (613) 135 0700
e-mail:	hertzloreto@msn.com

Edgar Moncayo Campana - Manager

Who you gonna call:

Airport:	135 - 0555
Ambulance:	135 - 1566
Bank:	135 - 0315
Bus Depot:	135 - 0767
City Hall:	135 - 0036
Customs at airport:	135 - 1266
Fire Department:	135 - 1566
Hospital:	135 - 0039
Highway patrol:	133 - 0794
Marine park:	135 - 1429
Police:	135 - 0035
Red Cross:	135 - 1111
Tourist info:	01 - 800 - 90 - 392 Toll free from Mex.

The Villages of Loreto Bay

Special Promotional Section

live fully . tread lightly

THE VILLAGES OF
LORETO BAY
live fully. tread lightly.

LORETO BAY

In one simple word, Loreto Bay is enchanting. It is the tranquil and serene Mexico of years past. Gaze down the long stretches of gorgeous sandy beaches and you will find calm, clear, blue water. Kayakers, anglers and snorkelers share the water with dolphins, whales and sea lions.

Jacques Cousteau called this stretch of the Sea of Cortés "the World's aquarium," as it offers abundant and diverse underwater sea life you could've only dreamt of before experiencing it for yourself.

Or, look to the sky and become captivated with the spectacular Sierra de la Giganta mountain range. Hike along the crest of the hilltops and catch a sunrise or sunset so stunning it will be emblazoned in your memory forever.

And the people — the people redefine hospitality. The culture and history of this peaceful town echo through the streets. Everyone is welcome to enjoy Loreto.

All in all, it's a wonderful town with all the appeal of the Baja lifestyle.

THE VILLAGES OF LORETO BAY

The Villages of Loreto Bay is an authentic Mexican seaside community in Baja California Sur.

The Loreto Bay Company in partnership with FONATUR, Mexico's tourism development agency, is constructing this community according to the principles of sustainable development. In fact, it is the largest and most ambitious sustainable development under construction in North America.

Approximately 200 miles north of La Paz, Loreto was identified by FONATUR almost 25 years ago as a prime tourism destination. In the years since, FONATUR has developed Cancun, Los Cabos, Ixtapa-Zihuatenejo and Huatulco and now, it is Loreto's turn. But there is something far different in store for this charming fishing village.

The Villages of Loreto Bay is a 15-year, $3 billion sustainable development project. This special place between the Sea of Cortés and the Sierra de la Giganta mountain range has become the canvas for amazing homes and 5-star amenities

– but all the while embracing an unprecedented sensitivity to the original landscape.

The property totals 8,000 acres, including more than three miles of beachfront. Of this land, 3,000 acres will be developed as a mixed-use, health-oriented seaside community of walkable villages. The remaining 5,000 acres will be maintained as a natural preserve ideal for hiking, cycling, horseback riding, organic farming and other activities.

Upon completion, The Villages of Loreto Bay will include 6,000 homes, hotels, service and retail businesses, and recreational facilities such as the Loreto Bay Golf Club, Beach Club and spas.

LORETO BAY
BAJA MEXICO

live fully . tread lightly

THE VILLAGES OF LORETO BAY

live fully. tread lightly.

NEIGHBORHOOD & HOMES

The homes of The Villages of Loreto Bay are being built in an environmentally sensitive place of spectacular natural beauty and are designed to reflect the local charm as well as the easy pace and flow of Baja, Mexico.

The year-round temperate climate welcomes indoor/outdoor living. The homes, which vary in floor plan, all feature many elements of traditional Colonial Mexican design: private interior courtyards, provision for shade and creative use of natural materials. The architecture gives the streetscape an authentic, artisanal feel.

The custom home division can work with you to design your dream vacation home, such as a custom-built beach-front or golf course villa. Or you can select one of the expressive floor plans for a condominium or Village Home. There are numerous sizes and styles, with prices starting in the low $200,000s (USD).

LORETO BAY
·BAJA MEXICO·

NEW URBANISM PRINCIPLES

At The Villages of Loreto Bay, everything needed is there, and everything there is needed. The quality of life at The Villages of Loreto Bay is in the sum of small things that make a daily difference as to how people live.

The design is that of an authentic pedestrian-friendly village. Landscaped walkways lined with homes and dotted with public spaces create a broader sense of belonging, welcoming you to join this burgeoning community. It is a place you can call both your community and your home.

Proposed amenities including village centers, beach club and golf club will all be within walking distance. Shape, color, proportion, harmony and architectural integrity create a community that joins extraordinary planning and soul-stirring architecture with culture and context.

THE VILLAGES OF
LORETO BAY
live fully. tread lightly.

LORETO BAY SPA, BEACH CLUB AND OTHER RECREATIONAL AMENITIES

Recreation and relaxation come in many forms for residents and guests of Loreto Bay. World-class recreational amenities offer something of interest for every member of your family.

Enriching your body, spirit, mind and appreciation of nature's blessing will be as simple as walking out your front door.

The proposed Town Center, lined with shops, restaurants and entertainment, will form the centerpiece of our pedestrian-friendly community.

The Beach Club, breaking ground in early 2005, will feature an acre of pools, a fitness center, a luxury hotel, and casual dining and catering facilities.

Stress melts away at the proposed world-class Spa where you will be able to enjoy a massage, steam and sauna, whirlpools, deep cleansing facials, natural body wraps and salon services.

Currently you'll find the Loreto Bay Golf Club, under redesign by PGA tour professional David Duval, and a Tennis Center that offers stadium seating for 250 fans.

The Villages of Loreto Bay are committed to the traditions and attractive way of life in Baja California Sur, Mexico. In order to preserve these customs, the Loreto Bay Company will present opportunities to participate in cultural programs and learn from notable speakers. Visitors and residents will enjoy the opportunity to attend authentic Mexican workshops, craft shows, film and other festivals, which are designed to inspire those who participate to ignite their own creative impulses.

Here at The Villages of Loreto Bay, the natural beauty and splendor of the Baja is yours to enjoy including three miles of beaches, horseback riding, casual and destination hiking, kayaking, deep-sea fishing, scuba diving, whale watching and more.

LORETO BAY GOLF CLUB

In addition to all the great amenities previously described, there will also be the first North American David Duval Signature Course at the Loreto Bay Golf Club. The course will be redesigned by championship golfer David Duval's golf course architecture firm, Duval Design.

Situated along three miles of beachfront on the Sea of Cortès, the Loreto Bay Golf Club is an 18-hole course which provides golfers with an open, welcoming environment that emphasizes strategic play and rewards risk takers.

The front nine will feature a links-style layout, including two dramatic holes hugging the Sea of Cortés. The back nine curves around an area where the mountains, sea and estuary meet, bringing several hazards into play. The signature 14th hole is a daunting par three, with an elevated tee shot over the sea to a green nestled on the beach in front of the rock outcropping defining the southern border of The Villages of Loreto Bay.

Duval Design will be renovating the course which was originally designed by noted Mexican golf course architect Pedro Guereca. The renovations, expected to be completed in 2006, will bring Loreto Bay Golf Club to current championship golf course standards. The par 72 course is expected to play at 7,200 yards from the Championship tees. After renovation, the course will be managed by Troon Golf, the world leader in golf course management of premier clubs and resort courses. The current Clubhouse will be renovated over the next two years, and there are also plans to open a golf school.

The Loreto Bay Golf Club will be a natural extension of the environment featuring native plants and seaside vegetation and will implement principles of sustainable development including the use of renewable energy sources and reclaimed water. The course will also use eco-focused management systems, including the use of paspallum grass, a saline-hardy hybrid grass developed for low-water usage.

THE VILLAGES OF
LORETO BAY

live fully. tread lightly.

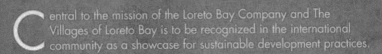

SUSTAINABILITY

Central to the mission of the Loreto Bay Company and The Villages of Loreto Bay is to be recognized in the international community as a showcase for sustainable development practices.

Within a long list of sustainability objectives are three cornerstone positions: Loreto Bay will harvest more potable water than it consumes, through re-use, groundwater retention and desalinizaation; Loreto Bay will create, through solar power and other means, more energy than it uses; Loreto Bay will enhance the habitat and nurture the bio-diversity of the land it occupies.

The overall commitment of the project is to develop land according to the United Nations' Brundtland Commission's definition: "meeting the needs of the present generation without sacrificing the ability of future generations to meet their own needs."

This commitment to sustainability will be accomplished through, but not limited to, the following points:

- Establishment of 5,000 acres of a natural preserve, including the mouth of the Primer Agua river and a significant portion of its watershed.
- Creation of pedestrian-oriented, bike-friendly and car-free neighborhoods with the use of photovoltaic powered electric carts as primary transportation.
- Fifty percent reduction of energy consumption through passive solar design and ground source heat.
- Generating more energy from renewable resources than consumed by the completion of the project.
- One hundred percent utilization of reclaimed water from effluent for irrigation.
- Introduction of a solid waste reduction program for recycling wherever possible and creation of facilities for composting one hundred percent of organic waste.
- Establishment of Perma-culture, organic farming and organic orcharding being an integral part of the development.
- Job creation programs within the community that will provide 2,000 jobs during construction and 5,000 permanent jobs in hospitality, local businesses, eco-tourism, agri-

culture, local manufacturing, the arts and artisan fields.

To move toward sustainability, it is important to set specific measurable performance standards that can be reproduced for other projects. We have drafted standards based on our previous experience to ensure that Loreto Bay will become the international model for sustainable tourism development.

CONCLUSION

I f you could live in any kind of community, surrounded by any kind of landscape, living as part of any kind of neighborhood, what would it be like?

This is what we came up with: it would have a pleasant climate with warm ocean water to swim in all year round; it would be a healthy environment with rich recreational opportunities; and it would be designed and built in such a way as to enhance, rather than degrade, the ecosystem. It would be a place where we would enjoy casual contact with our neighbors, who would be a diverse, interesting group and a pleasure to get to know.

This is The Villages of Loreto Bay.

As we continue to develop homes and amenities for residents and visitors to enjoy, we will continue to strengthen and preserve the local community and natural environment. This unique charm will undoubtedly draw many people to experience for themselves the appeal of this tranquil Baja town which redefines the meaning of natural beauty, culture and hospitality.

For more information on Loreto Bay's priority registration program, including upcoming Selection Event Weekends in Loreto , please call us toll free at 1.86 MYLORETO (1.866.956.7386) or visit www.LoretoBay.com.

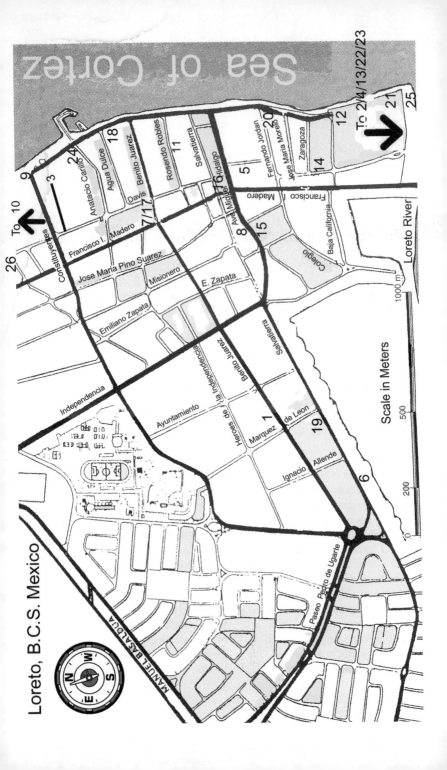

Loreto, B.C.S. Mexico

Sea of Cortez

Scale in Meters

Loreto River

MANUEL BASALDUA
Paseo Pedro de Ugarte

Constituyentes
Anatacio Carrillo
Agua Dulce
Benito Juarez
Rosendo Robles
Salvatierra
Hidalgo
Davis
Francisco I. Madero
Jose Maria Pino Suarez
Misionero
Emiliano Zapata
E. Zapata
Independencia
Ayuntamiento
Heroes de la Independencia
Benito Juarez
Marquez
de Leon
Ignacio Allende
Salvatierra
Ave. Miguel
Madero
Francisco
Baja California
Colegio
Fernando Jordan
Jose Maria Morelo
Zaragoza
To 10
26
9
3
24
18
7
17
16
8
15
5
20
11
12
14
21
25
1
19
6
2

To 2/4/13/22/23

Hotel Map

1 Motel Brenda
2 Camino Real
3 Coco Cabanas
4 Danzante
5 Motel El Dorado
6 Hacienda Suites
7 Iguana Inn
8 Hotel Junipero
9 Hotel La Pinta
10 Loreto Playa
11 El Moro Motel & R.V. Park
12 Hotel Oasis
13 Olive Tree Villas

14 Hotel Palmas Altas
15 Hotel Plaza Loreto
16 Hotel Posada de las Flores
17 Hotel Posada San Martin
18 Hotel Quinta San Francisco
19 Motel Salvatierra
20 Sukasa Bungalows
21 Villas de Loreto
22 Whales Inn
23 El Tripui R.V. Park
24 Loreto Hideaway
25 Loreto Shores
26 Riviera del Mar

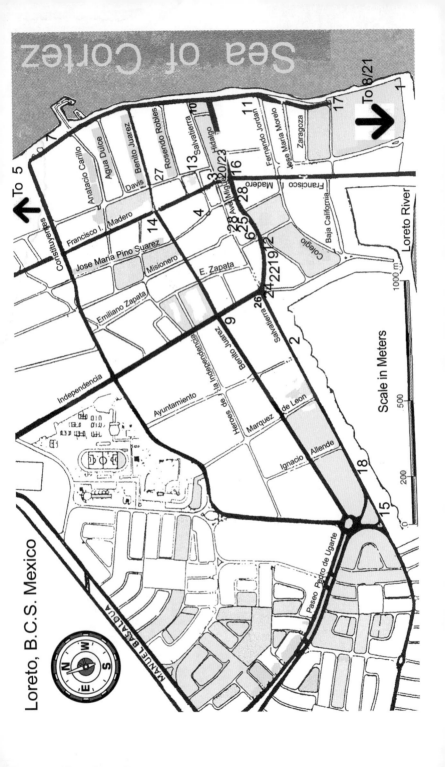

Loreto, B.C.S. Mexico

Sea of Cortez

Scale in Meters

Loreto River

Restaurant Map

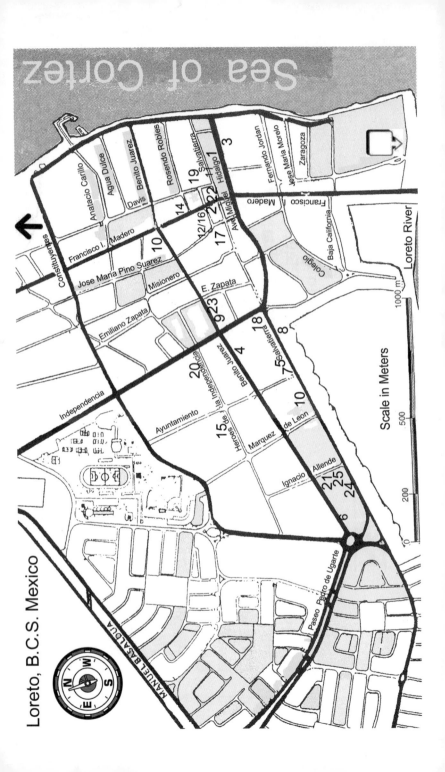

Loreto, B.C.S. Mexico

Sea of Cortez

Scale in Meters

Miscellaneous Map

1 Arturo's Sportfishing
2 Bank
3 Budget Car Rental
4 Cafe Internet Rene
5 Caseta Soledad Internet
6 Compu.- mas.com
7 Farmacia de las Californias
8 Farmacia del Rosario
9 Farmacia del Rosario #2
10 Farmacia Flores
11 Hertz Rental Car
12 Loreto Tourism Office
14 Library

15 Manni's Bicycle Shop
16 Municipal Building
17 Our Lady of Loreto Mission
18 El Pescador Supermarket
19 Central Plaza
20 Pool Hall
21 Post Office
22 .Com Internet
23 Ram 64 Internet
24 Red Cross
25 Telegraph / Money Transfer Office

<u>Notes</u>

Notes

Do you need assistance writing a book or want a book written for you?

We have a full time staff working to create the next generation of Riley Media books, but they also take on projects from outside our walls.

We can put together biographies, corporate histories or guides to your city.

Starting at $12,500, your idea can be turned into a paperback or e-book with thoroughly researched coverage of whatever topic you are interested in.

Email for information or a bid at mail@rileybooks.com

Coming in 2005

"You Decide Travel Guide: San Felipe"
"You Decide Travel Guide: La Paz"
"You Decide Travel Guide: Ensenada"
"You Decide Travel Guide: Mulege"
"You Decide Travel Guide: Rosarito Beach"